THIS COLORING BOOK BELONG TO

TEST COLOR PAGE

NEVER BE
limited By
Other People's
limited
IMAGINATIONS

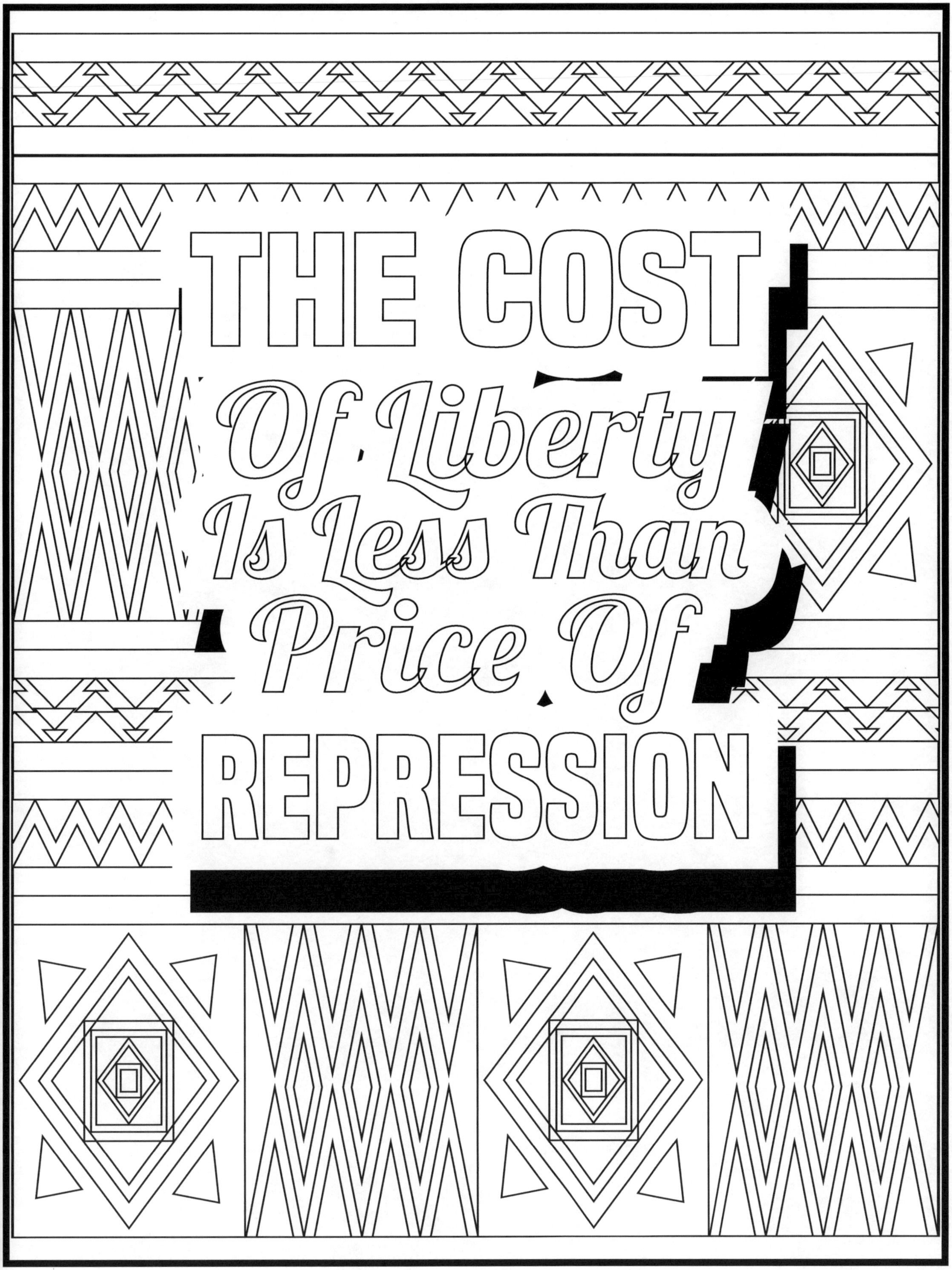
THE COST
Of Liberty
Is Less Than
Price Of
REPRESSION

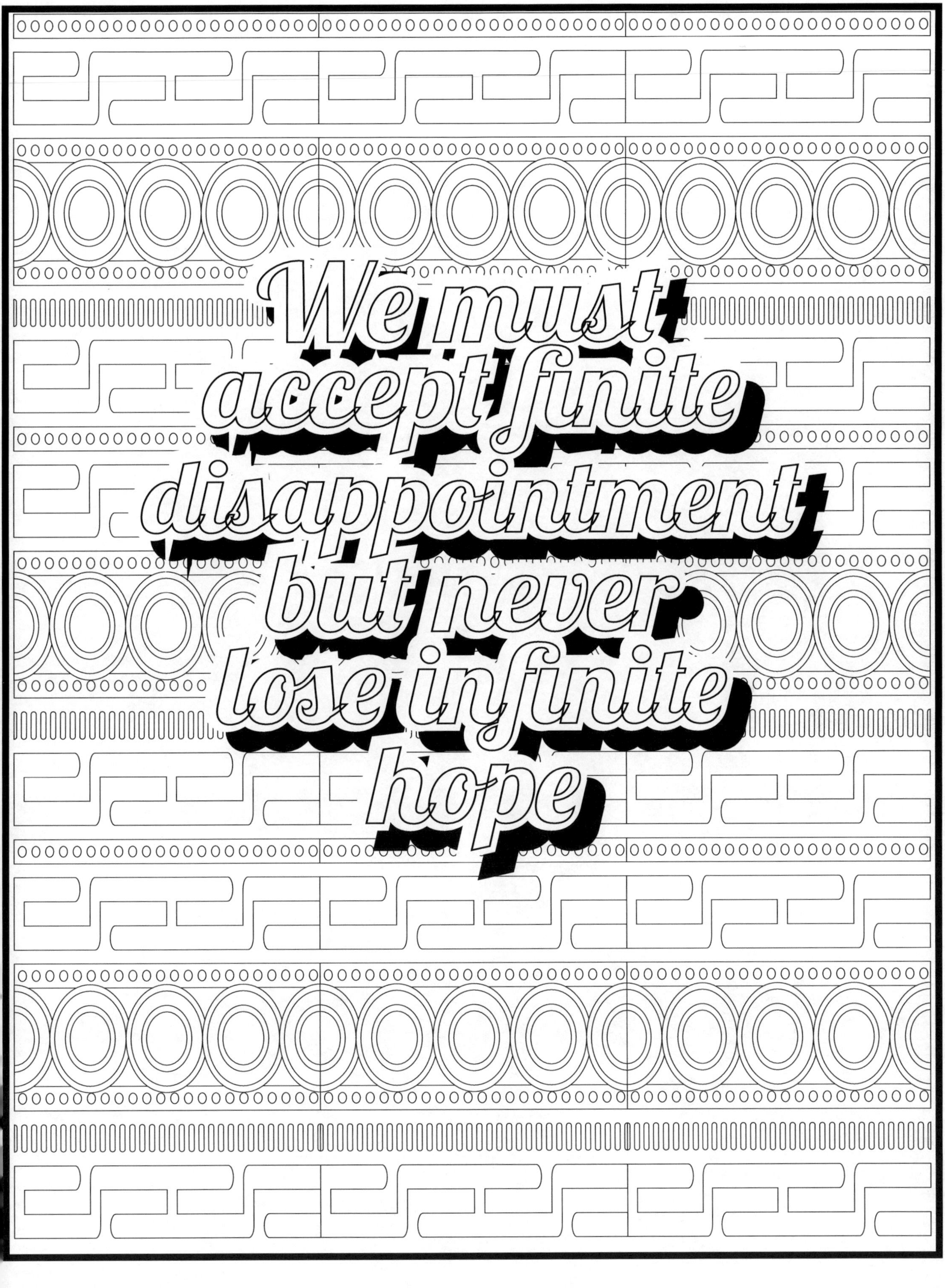
We must accept finite disappointment but never lose infinite hope

FORGIVENESS
is not an
occasional
act
It is a
permanent
ATTITUDE

NEVER
succumb
to the
temptation
of
BITTERNESS

Gave LIGHT
and people
WILL find
the way

Character
is
Power

If
there is no
struggle
there is no
progress

THE TIME IS
ALWAYS
RIGHT TO DO
WHAT IS
RIGHT

Freedom
IS NEVER
GIVEN
IT IS WON

Have
a vision be
demanding

TRUTH is
Powerful
and it
Prevails

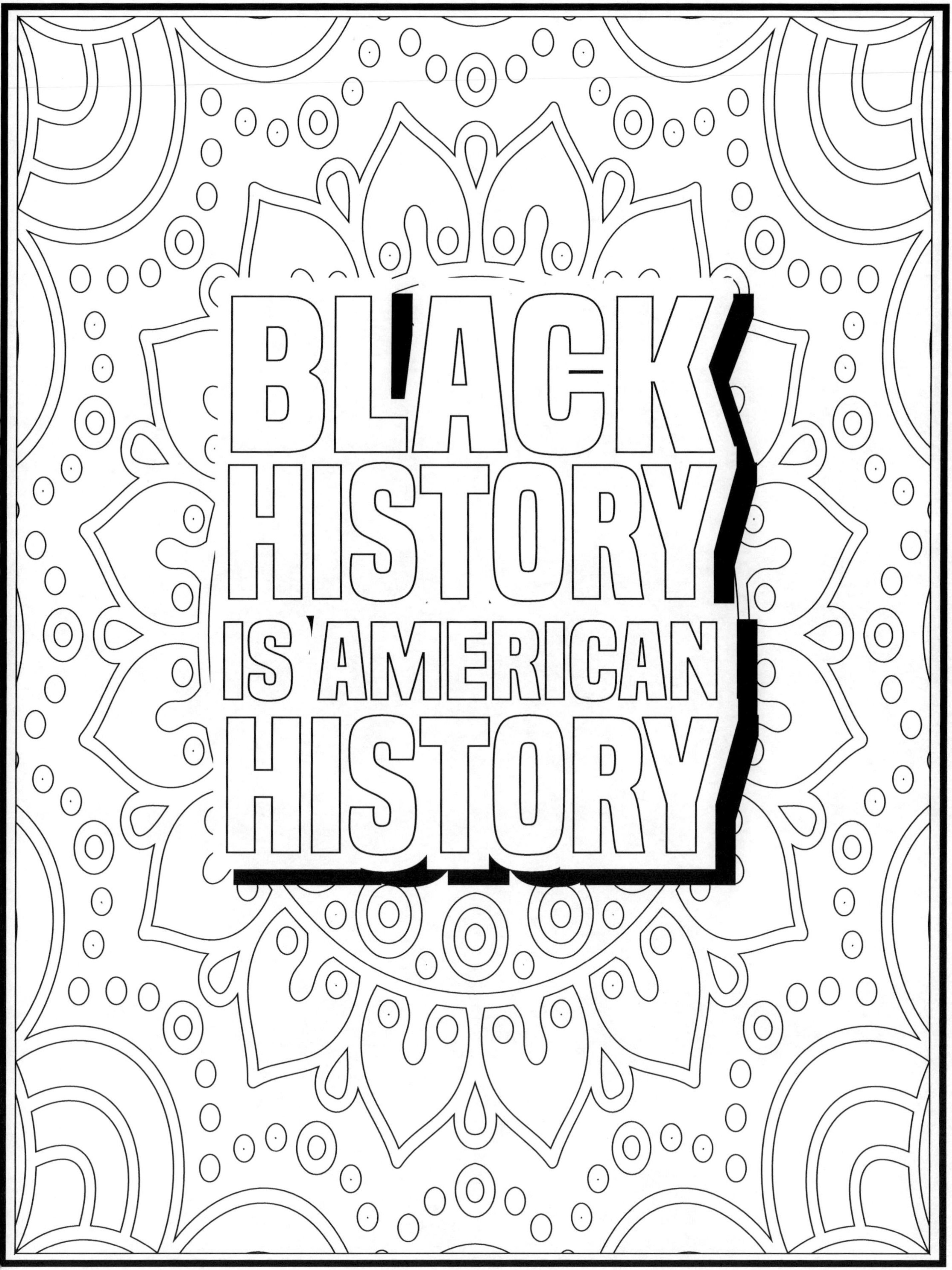
BLACK HISTORY IS AMERICAN HISTORY

THE SOUL
that is
within me
no man
can
DEGRADE

DON'T
AGONIZE
ORGANIZE

STRETCH
your mind
and fly

Be
as you are
and hope
that's right

YOU are YOUR BEST thing

EMBRACE
what makes you
UNIQUE
even if it makes
OTHERS
uncomfortable

Make a difference about something other than yourselves

The best way
TO MAKE
YOUR DREAMS
come
true is
to wake up

INJUSTICE
ANYWHERE
IS A THREAT
TO JUSTICE
EVERYWHERE

A good head
&
a good heart
are always
a formidable
combination

THERE IS NO
VACCINE
FOR RACISM

ACTIVISM
is my rent
for living
on the planet

NEVER
succumb to the
temptation of
BITTERNESS

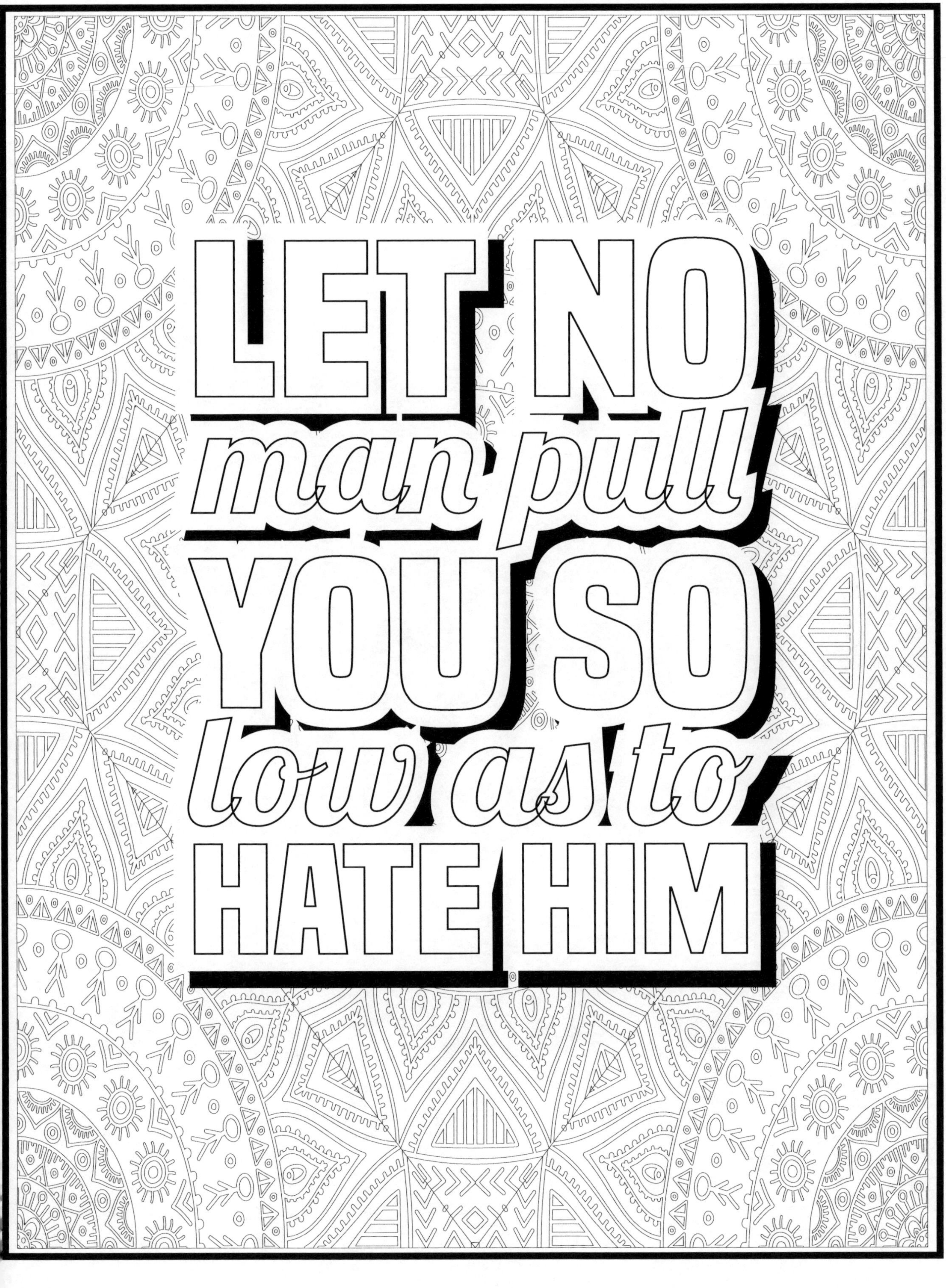
LET NO
man pull
YOU SO
low as to
HATE HIM

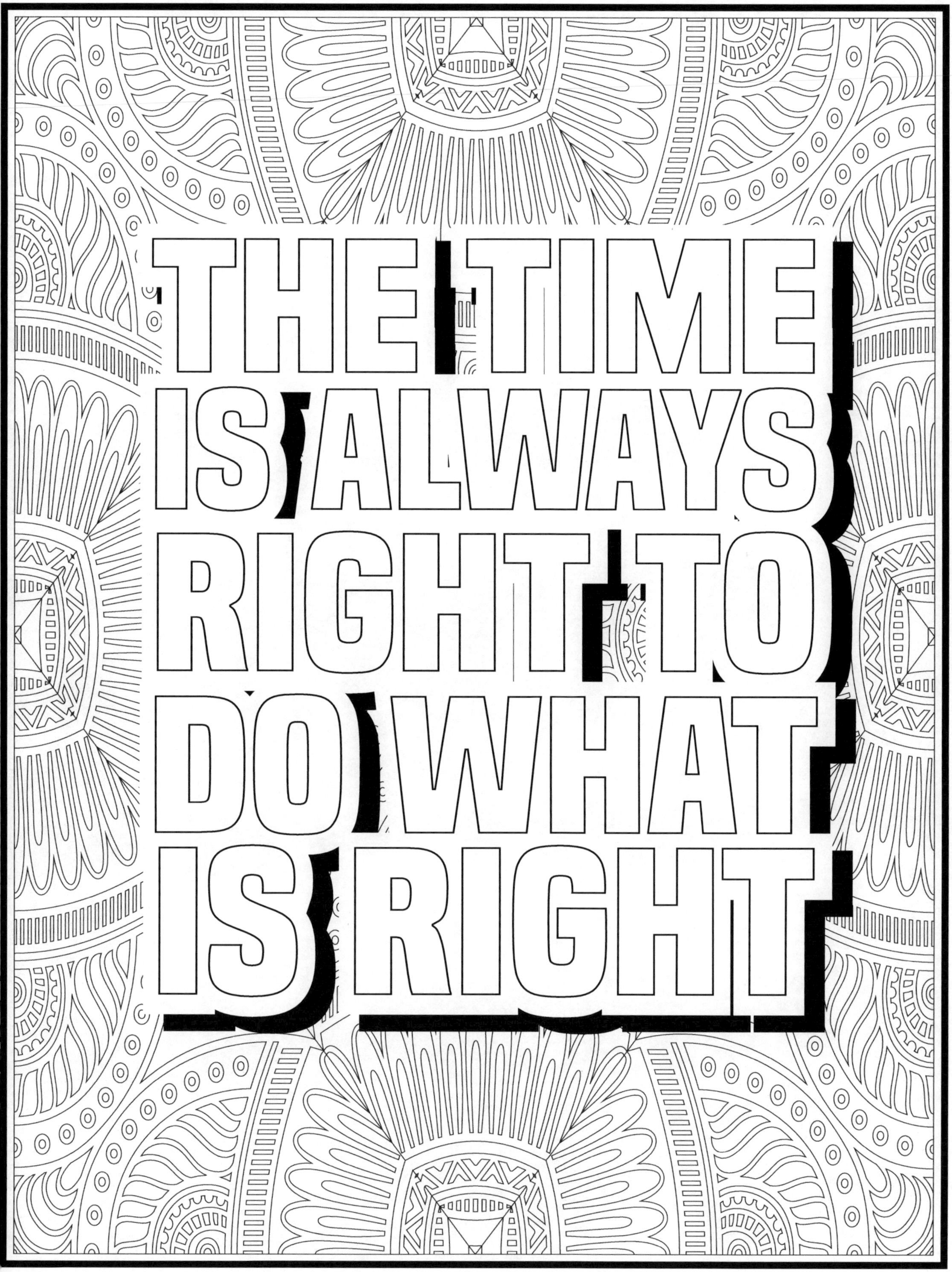
THE TIME IS ALWAYS RIGHT TO DO WHAT IS RIGHT

Made in the USA
Monee, IL
01 February 2024

52754960R00035